Fast Facts About Bugs & Spiders

Fast Facts About
SPIDERS

by Julia Garstecki

PEBBLE
a capstone imprint

Pebble Emerge is published by Pebble, an imprint of Capstone.
1710 Roe Crest Drive, North Mankato, Minnesota 56003
www.capstonepub.com

Copyright © 2021 by Capstone. All rights reserved. No part of this publication may be reproduced in whole or in part, or stored in a retrieval system, or transmitted in any form or by any means, electronic, mechanical, photocopying, recording, or otherwise, without written permission of the publisher.

Library of Congress Cataloging-in-Publication Data
Names: Garstecki, Julia, author.
Title: Fast facts about spiders / by Julia Garstecki.
Description: North Mankato, MN : Pebble, an imprint of Capstone, [2021] | Series: Fast facts about bugs & spiders | Includes bibliographical references and index. | Audience: Ages 6–8 | Audience: Grades 2–3 | Summary: "Do you spy a silky web? A spider must be nearby! Young readers will get the fast facts on these eight-legged critters, including spider body parts, habitats, and life cycles. Along the way, they will also uncover surprising and fascinating facts! Simple text, close-up photos, and a fun activity make this a perfect introduction to the spectacular world of spiders." —Provided by publisher.
Identifiers: LCCN 2020031926 (print) | LCCN 2020031927 (ebook) | ISBN 9781977131539 (hardcover) | ISBN 9781977132703 (paperback) | ISBN 9781977154217 (pdf) | ISBN 9781977155924 (kindle edition)
Subjects: LCSH: Spiders—Juvenile literature.
Classification: LCC QL458.4 .G37 2021 (print) | LCC QL458.4 (ebook) | DDC 595.4/4—dc23
LC record available at https://lccn.loc.gov/2020031926
LC ebook record available at https://lccn.loc.gov/2020031927

Image Credits
Shutterstock: Abigail Barhorst, 5, Cristian Gusa, cover, D. Kucharski K. Kucharska, 7, Dwi Yulianto, 16, guentermanaus, 18, Insago, 20 (color paper), Inspiration GP, 20 (bottom left), Leonid Ikan, 12, Matauw, 14, Mega Pixel, 20 (middle right), Nenad Nedomacki, 4, Piboon Suwankosai, 13, PJ photography, 11, Pong Wira, 17, Sandra Standbridge, 10, SeDmi, 20 (middle left), SweetLemons, 20 (top right), thatmacroguy, 15, Vasilius, 20 (top left), Viktor Loki, 19, withthesehands, 9, zabavina (background), cover and throughout, Zzzenia, 21

Editorial Credits
Editor: Abby Huff; Designer: Hilary Wacholz; Media Researcher: Jo Miller; Production Specialist: Tori Abraham

All internet sites appearing in back matter were available and accurate when this book was sent to press.

Table of Contents

Words in **bold** are in the glossary.

All About Spiders

Look! Do you see a web? A spider must be nearby. More than 35,000 kinds live in the world. Most spiders are black or brown. They can also be green, red, and yellow.

Spiders live almost everywhere. Some live in deserts or forests. Others live in water. But they do not live in Antarctica. It's too cold there.

Spiders are **arachnids**. They have two body sections. They have eight legs. Many spiders also have eight eyes. Others see with six or fewer.

Spiders have tiny hairs on their bodies. The hairs smell and taste. Hairs on their feet stick to things. This lets the spider walk upside down!

eye

hair

legs

Special Silk

All spiders make silk. It comes out of body parts called **spinnerets**. Spiders make different kinds of silk. It can be thick or thin. It can be sticky or strong.

Spiders use silk in many ways. Some use it to make webs. Some wrap **prey** in it. All spiders can drop from high places using silk. Others use silk to fly in the wind!

spinneret

A Spider's Life

A female spider lays eggs. She wraps them in silk. This is called an egg sac. Some females carry the sac. Some keep it in their web. Others hide it.

egg sac

Soon the eggs hatch. The young are called spiderlings. They look like tiny adults. They **molt** as they grow. Some spiders live for a year. Others live for 20 years!

Dinnertime!

Spiders eat lots of **insects**. Some snack on other spiders too. Big spiders can eat big animals. These include frogs, snakes, and birds.

A spider bites prey with two **fangs**. The fangs shoot out **venom**. This liquid kills prey. Then the spider spits up stomach juice. It turns food to mush. The spider sucks it up.

fangs

Spiders are great **predators**. Many use silk to catch food. Some make webs. The webs can be big or small. They come in different shapes.

One web is shaped like a circle. It hangs between plants. It's hard to see. An insect flies into the web. It gets stuck in the sticky silk. Time for the spider to eat!

Not all spiders use webs to catch meals. Some hunt! Jumping spiders hunt like cats. They spot a bug. They sneak up on it. Then, hop! They jump on the bug.

Trapdoor spiders dig holes. They make a cover of silk and dirt. It blends into the ground. The spiders wait in the hole. They grab insects that walk by.

Fun Facts

- Spiders eat millions of insects a year. This helps farmers and gardeners.

- The smallest spiders can fit on top of a pin. The biggest are tarantulas. Some grow almost 1 foot (0.3 meters) long!

tarantula

black widow spider

- Some spiders look like bird poop. Then animals don't eat them!

- Venom from a black widow spider can make people sick. But most spider bites don't hurt people.

Make a Spider

What You Need:

- paint or markers
- four craft sticks
- glue
- colored paper
- scissors
- googly eyes

What You Do:

1. Paint or color the craft sticks.

2. To make the spider's legs, glue one stick on top of another. It should look like an X. Repeat until all sticks are glued together.

3. Cut a circle from the paper. This is the body. Glue it where all the sticks cross. Then glue googly eyes to the paper.

Glossary

arachnid (uh-RAK-nid)—an animal with a hard outer shell, eight legs, and two body sections

fang (FANG)—a long, pointed toothlike mouthpart

insect (IN-sekt)—a small animal with a hard outer shell, six legs, three body sections, and two antennae

molt (MOLT)—to shed an outer layer of skin

predator (PRED-uh-tur)—an animal that hunts other animals for food

prey (PRAY)—an animal hunted by another animal for food

spinneret (spin-uh-RET)—a part found on the end of a spider's body that squirts out silk

venom (VEN-uhm)—a liquid made by some animals that can hurt or kill other animals

Read More

Higgins, Melissa. *Splendid Spiders: A 4D Book.* North Mankato, MN: Pebble, 2020.

Murray, Julie. *Tarantula Spiders.* Minneapolis: Abdo Publishing, 2020.

Parker, Steve. *Insects and Spiders.* New York, DK Publishing, 2019.

Internet Sites

DK Find Out!: Spiders
dkfindout.com/us/animals-and-nature/invertebrates/spiders/

National Geographic Kids: Tarantula
kids.nationalgeographic.com/animals/invertebrates/tarantula/

Pest World for Kids: Spiders
pestworldforkids.org/pest-guide/spiders/

Index